Written

Just for you

Copyright ©, Kate Green, 2025
All rights reserved. No parts of this book may be copied, distributed, or published in any form without permission from the publisher.
For permissions contact: katie80green@gmail.com
This is a work of fiction in which all events and characters in this book are completely imaginary. Any resemblance to actual people is entirely coincidental.
ISBN: 978-0-6457171-9-8
Published by Kate Green katie80green@gmail.com
and https://kate-green-106256.square.site

Meet Yetti, a curious little explorer who reminds us about the power of yet —because even when things seem tricky, they know they're just not there yet!

Yetti was a little explorer with BIG ideas! They loved trying new things and
...finding creative ways to use ordinary objects

One day, they decided to build the tallest tower in the forest.
They stacked sticks, stones,
and even a pancake (leftover from breakfast).

Wobble... wobble...

"Oh well." Yetti said with a smile. "I just don't have it yet!"

They dusted off their fur and ...

.....tried again.

Next. Yetti wanted to fly like the birds. They gathered leaves for wings and
made a helmet from a mixing bowl.

They climbed onto a tree stump, spread their arms, and...
WHOOSH! They flapped and fluttered...

.... right into a pile of soft moss.

"I guess I can't fly... yet!" they giggled. But they had another idea.

Yetti found an old wagon and turned it into a speedy zoom-mobile! "Wagons are for pulling." said their friend. Ollie the Owl.

"But what if... they were for zooming?" Yetti grinned, giving it a push. WHOOSH! Down the hill they went—until they landed in a pile of leaves.

"Almost!" they cheered. "I just haven't figured it out

... yet!"

Yetti's next big idea was to build a bridge across the creek using their skipping rope
and a few logs.
"Bridges aren't made from skipping ropes." said Jessie the Jackrabbit, very confused.

"But what if... they could be?"
      Yetti tied the rope tight and took a careful step—

until SPLASH! into the water they went.

They shook off the water and laughed. "Not quite... yet!"

As night fell, Yetti looked up at the stars. "I may not have built the tallest tower, or flown, or zoomed the fastest yet,

but I'll keep trying!"

They snuggled into their cozy nest of blankets, dreaming of new ideas. Tomorrow would be another day of exploring, imagining, and believing in the magic of yet!

Because with a little patience and a lot of heart, anything is possible...